CHAPTER FIVE

A BETTER TOMORROW

ACTION LAB DANGER ZONE PRESENTS

INFINITE 7

WRITTEN BY
DAVE DWONCH

DRAWN BY
ARTURO MESA

COLORED BY
GERALDO FILHO

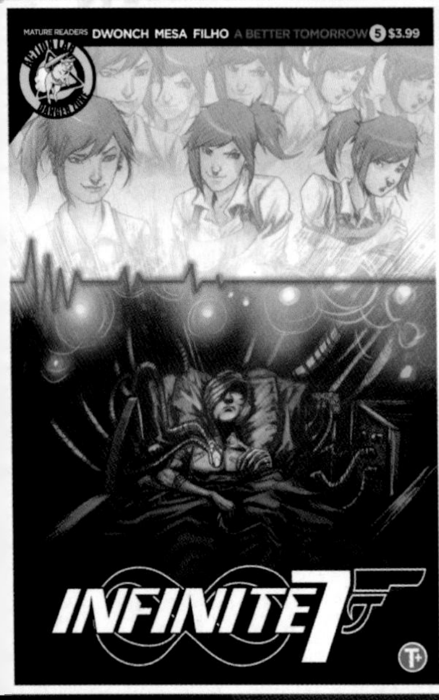

CVR A- REGULAR COVER
by Arturo Mesa

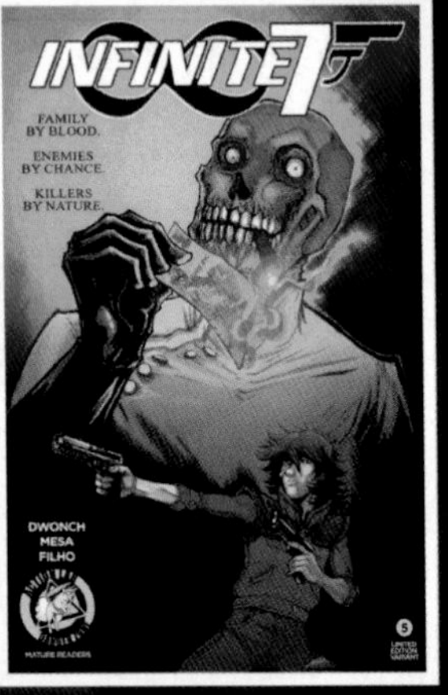

CVR B- MOVIE POSTER
by Arturo Mesa
Limited to 1,500 Copies

CVR C- ARTIST VARIANT
by Dave Dwonch
Limited to 1,500 Copies

LETTERED BY DAVE DWONCH

EDITED BY MEGAN DOBRANSKY AND SHAWN GABBORIN

THE STORY SO FAR:

During the assault on Chimera's hidden base, Anthony Zane's parents were revealed as the international terrorists, Madame Mavara and the Laughing Skull. In her escape, Mavara shot Anthony in the face, while the Laughing Skull was apprehended by the Infinite Seven. Now, Anthony clings to life in a coma...

Read Volume One Now!
APR171193

ACTION LABCOMICS.COM

JASON MARTIN - PUBLISHER
BRYAN SEATON - CEO
SHAWN PRYOR - PRESIDENT
SHAWN GABBORIN - EDITOR IN CHIEF
NICOLE D'ANDRIA - MARKETING MGR.
JIM DIETZ - SOCIAL MEDIA DIRECTOR
CHAD CICCONI - AGENT OF CHIMERA

INFINITE7
MICHAEL CALERO!

FRIEDRICH
NIETZSCHE
BEYOND
GOOD
AND

COVER GALLERY

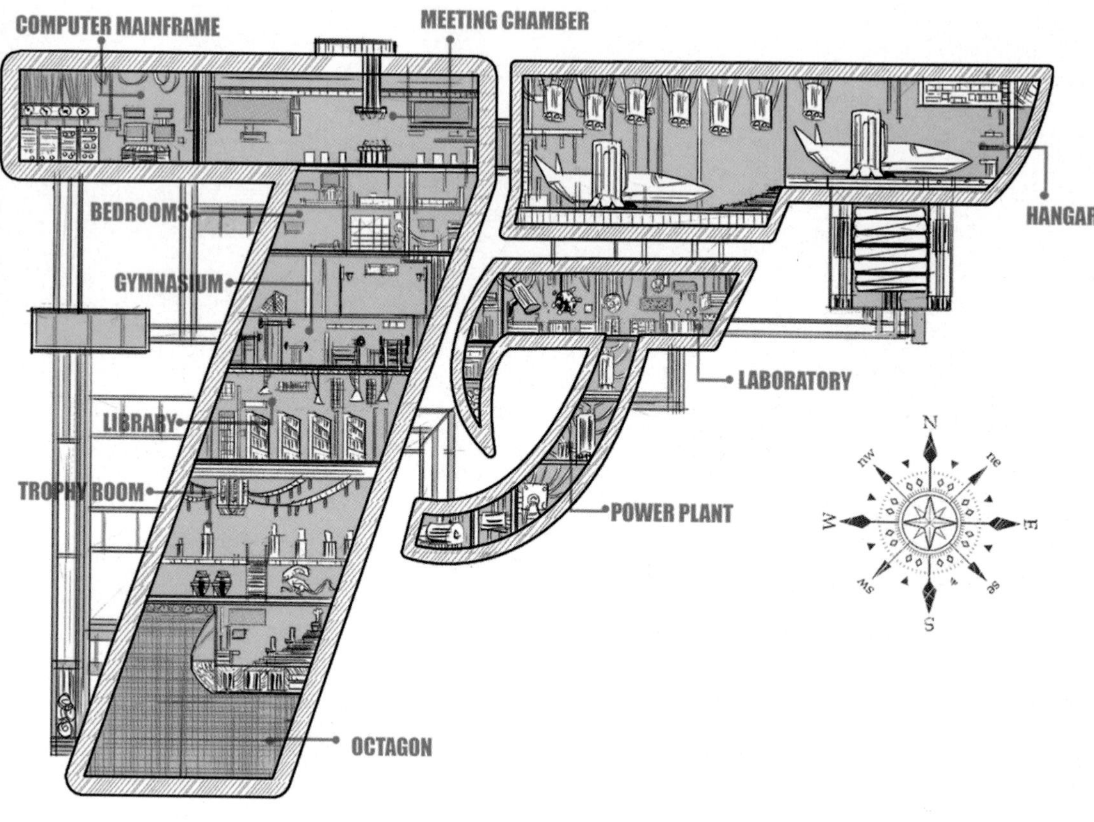

A: REGULAR COVER BY
ARTURO MESA & GERALDO FILHO

B: MOVIE POSTER VARIANT
BY ARTURO MESA & GERALDO FILHO

C: ARTIST VARIANT BY
MICHAEL CALERO & GERALDO FILHO

Afterwords

WOW. How was THAT for a CLIFFHANGER?

Arturo, Geraldo and I are super proud of this series and this issue in particular. All roads were leading here and I think we succeeded in delivering an action-packed season finale.

"SEASON FINALE?" you're probably asking yourself right about now.

Yes, Infinite Seven is going on a brief hiatus and will be relaunching with a new #1 issue for its second season. While Infinite Seven has been running as a monthly series for the most part, we've been at this for the better part of two years. We've all gotten faster, but keeping the monthly schedule has been ha We fell behind a bit in the wake of SDCC, but the con allowed for Arturo and I to meet for the first time and we were able to concoct the next batch of stories together over many, many beers. The future for the Infinite Seven is bright (or incredibly dark, I guess), but we need time to build up a reserve of issue so that we can deliver the next arc without interruption.

I'm also working on a new series, and a couple of returning titles.

Get ready for the long-awaited return of Space-Time Condominium and Double Jumpers!

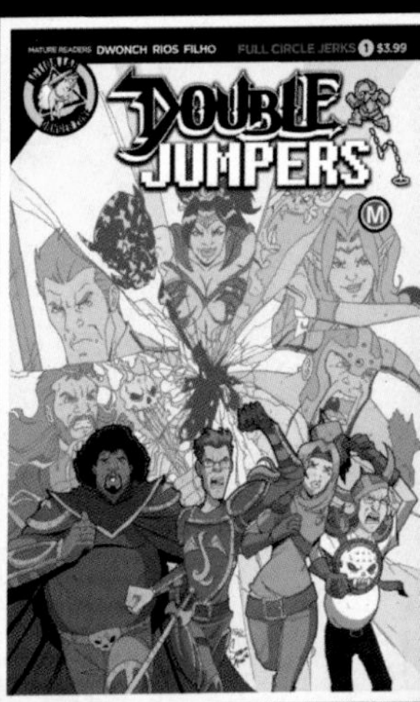

Along with my riff on the zombie genre in Prom of the Dead and a top-secret project Arturo and I are also developing, 2018 is looking to be a banner year for the team!

Look for Infinite Seven to return late next year.

In the meantime, tell your friends about Infinite Seven. With all the comics being published today it's incredibly difficult to find an audienc so spreading the good word is necessary and VERY appreciated.

We'll be back soon, and we hope you'll not only stick with us, but drag your friends into our brand of super spies and assassins.

Cheers,

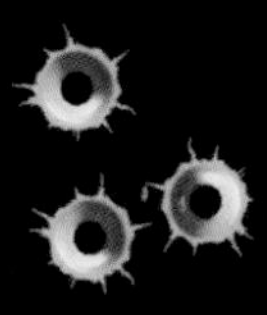

Dave Dwonch
From the cabin in the woods

NEXT: ONCE UPON A TIME IN MEXICO

I ONLY HOPE SOME OF THE OTHERS MADE IT OUT ALIVE.
I LOVED HIM. MY BROTHER. HE... I WORSHIPPED HIM.
I KNOW. WE GONNA MAKE CHIMERA PAY FOR TURNING HIM. BELIEVE THAT.
THOSE THAT DID NOT...
...GUH...GOD... SPEED, MY FRIENDS.
BA-DOOM
...WILL BE AVENGED.

...GODSPEED, MY FRIENDS.
FIVE MINUTES.
ZHEN! SHERLOCK! WE HAVE TO SAVE THEM!
THAT'S ALL IT TOOK FOR OUR WORLD TO TURN TO SHIT.
YOU CRAZY? WE GOTTA GET THE FUCK OUTTA HERE.
WE WERE AT WAR, AND NONE OF US WERE PREPARED FOR WHAT THAT TRULY MEANT.
ARE YOU READY TO GO?
HOW?
ONE OF SHERLOCK'S TELEPORTATION PILLS. YOU'RE FAMILIAR, NO?
NOT THE LOSS, THE *DEATH*, NO...
WE WERE *OLD LOVERS*. NO...
...WE WEREN'T PREPARED FOR *BETRAYAL*.
SOMEONE SET US UP, SIGNED OUR DEATH WARRANTS. LEFT US TO DIE.

NO.
GOODBYE, MY FRIENDS.
NO!!
COMPUTER, OVERRIDE CODE THX-1138. ACTIVATE SELF-DESTRUCT PROTOCOL.
AGENTS OF THE SHADOW CABINET. YOU HAVE THIRTY SECONDS TO MAKE YOUR ESCAPE.
SELF-DESTRUCT HAS BEEN ENGAGED ON MY AUTHORITY. TH
IS AGENT CINCO, SIGNING OFF...

I KNOW YOU'VE BEEN THROUGH HELL FIGURATIVELY--
--BUT IT'S TIME TO SHOW YOU WHAT HELL REALLY IS.
YARGHHH!
OH, MY GOD.
WHAT... WHAT... HAVE I...
HE MADE ME... DO THIS... HANS... BROTHER...
YOU GOTTA PULL IT TOGETHER, WOLFSBERG. WE-

ESCAPE?
YOU HAVE NO IDEA WHO YOU ARE DEALING WITH.
YOU'RE ALL GOING TO DIE HERE.
YOUR GODDAMN RIGHT, ZHEN.
THESE MOTHERFUCKAS GONNA PAY FOR COMING TO OUR HOUSE.
BLAM
WHO'S NEXT? OH, YEAH. YOU'LL DO.
PING!
PING!
PING!
PING!
BLAM
BLAM
BLAM
WE'D HOPED TO SAVE YOU, BUT YOU'VE PROVEN NOTHING MORE THAN A SOULLESS SHELL.

AGREED. DAD, CAN YOU WALK?
PATIENCE.
I- I think so, yes.
GOOD. MEET ME IN THE POWER PLANT. WE'RE GOING TO BLOW THIS PLACE TO HELL.
She really is something.
YEAH, SHE IS. HOLD ON.
ONE FOR THE ROAD.
BLAM
You've really come into your own, son.
THAT'S WHAT EVERYONE KEEPS TELLING ME.
"THERE IS NO ESCAPE!"

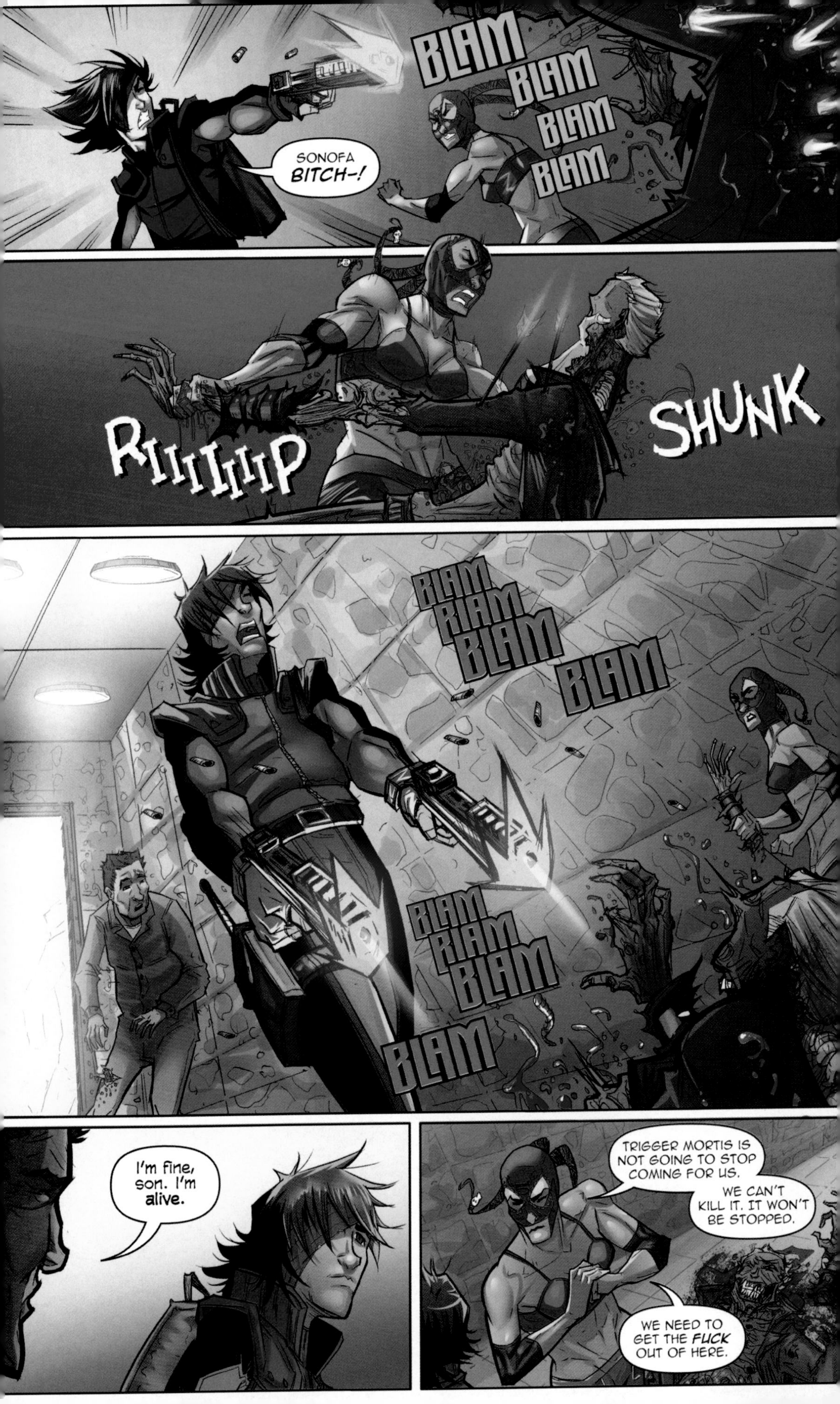

BLAM
BLAM
BLAM
BLAM
SONOFA *BITCH-!*

RIIIIIIIP
SHUNK

BLAM
BLAM
BLAM
BLAM
BLAM
BLAM
BLAM
BLAM

I'm fine, son. I'm **alive.**

TRIGGER MORTIS IS NOT GOING TO STOP COMING FOR US.
WE CAN'T KILL IT. IT WON'T BE STOPPED.
WE NEED TO GET THE *FUCK* OUT OF HERE.

Yes... yes. We're in terrible danger.
...terrible... danger...
GUN!
DAD!
BLAM

--KILL YOU. THEY ARE GOING TO GUT YOU LIKE A FISH.
Shut up shut up shut up!
Get out of my head!

TSK. I'M THE ONLY THING THAT CAN SAVE YOU, IDIOT. WHEN THE OPPORTUNITY PRESENTS ITSELF, ALL YOU NEED DO IS GIVE YOURSELF TO ME, RUTHERFORD...

...I'LL SAVE US BOTH.
DAD! WE'VE GOT TO GET OUT OF HERE!
HELLO, "SON." WHAT... WHAT'S GOING ON?

Hello, son. What... what's going on?
THEY'RE HERE. CHIMERA.
OH, GOD DAMN IT.

I'M SURE THEY'RE HERE FOR YOU.
IT'S ONLY A MATTER OF MINUTES BEFORE THEY ARE ON TOP OF US. WE'VE GOT TO MOVE.

BOSS!
WOLFSBERG!

ZZZZT
DON' SAY I NEVER DID NUTHIN FOR YA!

YOU SOULLESS BASTARD. HE WAS ME BEST MATE! YOU'RE GOING TO-

-PAY. PAY FOR WHAT YOU PUT ME THROUGH.
WE'RE BROTHERS. DON'T MAKE... DON'T MAKE ME...

AND NOW I GOTTA DEAL WITH THIS PIECE OF SHIT.
I'M GOING TO ENJOY KILLIN YOU, BABY FUCKER.
BLAM BLAM BLAM
PING
GIVE IN, LITTLE BROTHER. YOU WERE NEVER MEANT TO REPLACE ME. SAY IT.
YOU ALWAYS WERE A STUBBORN FOOL, HANS. POPPA SAID-
POPPA WAS THE FOOL!
I'M STILL YOUR BETTER! I ALWAYS HAVE BEEN-!
SAY IT.
YARGHH--!

WE NEED TO BE
FAR, FAR AWAY
WHEN IT DOES."
THIS
SN'T
IGHT.
YOU
THINK?!
NO... THIS...
THIS IS JUST A
DISTRACTION. THEY'RE
HERE FOR MORE
THAN A FIGHT.
dad.
WHERE ARE
YOU GOING,
SMASH?
TO THE
HYDRAULIC
LIFT.
WHAT?
WHY?
IT'S A
SHORTCUT TO THE
HOLDING PENS
IN THE LAB.
YOU'RE
SURE ABOUT
THIS?
YEAH,
I'VE STUDIED THE
BLUEPRINTS BACKWARDS
AND FORWARD. IT'S A
TIGHT FIT, BUT IT'LL
GET US THERE
QUICKER.
LEAD
THE WAY.

"WHERE THE HELL *IS* HE?!"
I WAS WONDERING WHEN YOU'D SHOW UP.
WHAT WOULD THEY THINK IF THEY KNEW YOU BETRAYED THEM?
ONE WORD FROM ME AND THEY'D KNOW JUST WHAT KIND OF MONSTER THEIR LEADER IS.

YOU ALWAYS RELIED TOO MUCH ON DE GUN, LITTLE BROTHER.
GODDAMNIT!
CLICK
CLICK
CLICK
THIS COULD BE THE END, BOYS.
I FUCKING HATE YOU.
STAY POSITIVE, WASHINGTON. TEDDY HUXTABLE WILL LIVE TO SEE ANOTHER DAY.
BLAM BLAM BLAM
RIP HIM TO SHREDS, WATSON!
WHERE IS *ELLINGTON*? DOES ANYONE HAVE EYES ON *AGENT SEVEN*?!
BLAM

"I'LL MAKE SURE WE GET OUT OF HERE ALIVE."
LEMME RIP 'IS INNARDS OUT, BOSS!
YOU TOOK US BY SURPRISE LAST TIME, DEAR. I WON'T LET MY EMOTIONS GET THE BEST OF ME THIS TIME 'ROUND.

THE LIGHTS AREN'T GOING TO TURN THEMSELVES ON!"
kooom! kooom! kooom!
W-who... who's there?
WELL, AT LEAST THEY GOT THE LIGHTS TO WORK.
kooom!
NOW WE'LL BE ABLE TO SEE THEM COMING FOR US.
Chimera? Chimera is here?
YOU WERE NEVER THE BRIGHTEST STAR IN THE SKY. YES, THEY'RE HERE, MEATSKIN.
W-why-?
FOR ONE OF TWO REASONS: TO FREE US, OR MORE LIKELY... TO KILL US.
ONE THING'S FOR CERTAIN. WHEN IT COMES TIME TO FIND OUT, I'LL BE HERE TO PROTECT US.
JUST PUT ME ON AND I'LL DO THE REST.

OKAY, FINDING THE PROBLEM SHOULD BE...
SLAM
...NEXT TO... IMPOSSIBLE. THIS COULD TAKE A WHILE.
I DON'T HAVE TIME FOR THIS.
¡NO MAMES! WHAT KIND OF LUCK IS THAT?! WHO WOULD DO SOMETHING LIKE THIS? THIS-
THIS COULD ONLY HAVE BEEN AN INSIDE JOB, BUT WHO...
LATER. NOW IS NOT THE TIME. FOC ON THE TASK AT HAND.

"...LET'S CAUSE SOME BLOODY MAYHEM."
WHAT IN BLUE BLAZES IS GOING ON?
I'LL TELL YOU WHAT, WE'RE-
--UNDER ATTACK! CINCO IS HEADED TO THE MAINFRAME TO REBOOT THE SYSTEM AND, WAIT-
-IS THAT A TEDDY BEAR?
WHATCHU KNOW? THIS IS MY OG TEDDY HUXTABLE, MOTHERFUCKA. HAD HIM SINCE I WAS A KID.
I MEAN, IT'S A CHILD'S PLAYTHING. IT-
IT'S A COLLECTABLE!
ENOUGH!
WE DON'T HAVE TIME FOR THIS.
IT DOESN'T TAKE A GENIUS TO FIGURE OUT THAT CHIMERA IS BEHIND THIS.
YOU ALL NEED TO SUIT UP. THE WAR HAS BEGUN.

"WE HAVE BEEN BREACHED."

WHERE THE HELL ARE WE?

THE LIBRARY. THE MOUNTAIN FACE WAS THINNEST HERE. THEY THOUGHT IT IMPENETRABLE, BUT I KNEW BETTER.

DEMOLITIONS WERE ALWAYS YOUR SPECIALTY, OLD MAN.

OLD? YOU'RE ONE TO TALK.

I WEAR IT WELL. NOW LET'S GET TO BRASS TACKS.

IF THEY'RE SMART THEY'LL HEAD TO THE HANGAR--
BLOW THIS PLACE TO HELL, AND MAKE THEIR ESCAPE.
WE FINISH THEM THERE. NOW...

TRIGGER MORTIS. YOU HAVE YOUR ORDERS. THE REST OF YOU...

LEAVING YOU BREATHING IS A MISTAKE I WOULD NEVER HAVE MADE.
YOU'RE RIGHT. SHE'S NOT ONE TO LEAVE-
BA-DOOM
-LOOSE ENDS.
WHAT THE HELL WAS THAT?
SOMETHING I NEVER THOUGHT POSSIBLE, HERMANITO...

--*DEAD I'D BE.* SO YOU THINK-

THAT SHE PURPOSEFULLY LET YOU LIVE?

SLEAZE BAR
TEQUILA

COMPUTER, NEW LOCATION: TITTY TWISTER.

Affirmative. Loading...

KNOW
BOUT
OSS,
THONY.
SMASH.
YES, SMASH. I KNOW ABOUT LOSS. MY FATHER... MY ENTIRE FAMILY WAS MURDERED BY THE LAUGHING SKULL.

MY DAD, HE-
NOT YOUR DAD. THE THING THAT CONTROLLED HIM. TRUST ME, I'VE SPENT TIME WITH HIM. HE'S INNOCENT. UN PEÓN.
I WANTED TO HATE HIM. TO KILL HIM. BUT I CAN'T.

LISTEN, I'M REALLY SORRY ABOUT... ABOUT THE FIGHT. I REALLY LOST IT.

NONSENSE.
YOU DID WHAT YOU FELT WAS RIGHT. YOU'VE FOUND YOUR WAY IN A VERY SHORT TIME.
CLINK

FIVE MINUTES EARLIER.
YOU'RE GETTING BETTER.
YOU'RE GETTING SLOWER.
YOU KNOW WHAT WE SAY: IF I WANTED YOU DEAD, DEAD YOU'D BE.
WHAT DO YOU WANT?
TO TALK. EXPLAIN MYSELF. TO MAKE AMENDS.

WE HAD GROWN COMPLACENT.
WE NEVER SAW THEM COMING.
IN SHEER NUMBER, WE WERE OUTMATCHED.
ZHEN! SHERLOCK! WE HAVE TO SAVE THEM!
YOU CRAZY? WE GOTTA GET THE FUCK OUTTA HERE.
THERE WAS NO WAY TO WIN.
COMPUTER, OVERRIDE CODE THX-1138. ACTIVATE SELF-DESTRUCT PROTOCOL.
BUT WE WERE NOT GOING TO DIE IN VAIN.
BOOM!
WE WOULD TAKE THEM ALL WITH US, AND LET *HELL* SORT US OUT.
BOOM!
BOOM!

ACTION LAB DANGER ZONE PRESENTS

INFINITE 7

WRITTEN BY DAVE DWONCH
DRAWN BY ARTURO MESA
COLORED BY GERALDO FILHO

CVR A- REGULAR COVER
by Arturo Mesa

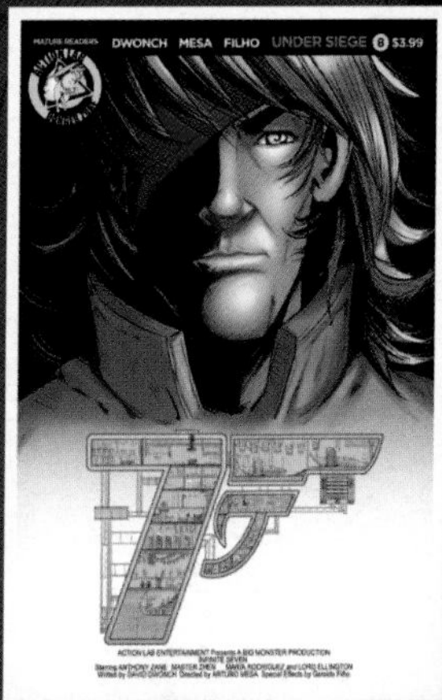

CVR B- MOVIE POSTER
by Arturo Mesa
Limited to 1,500 Copies

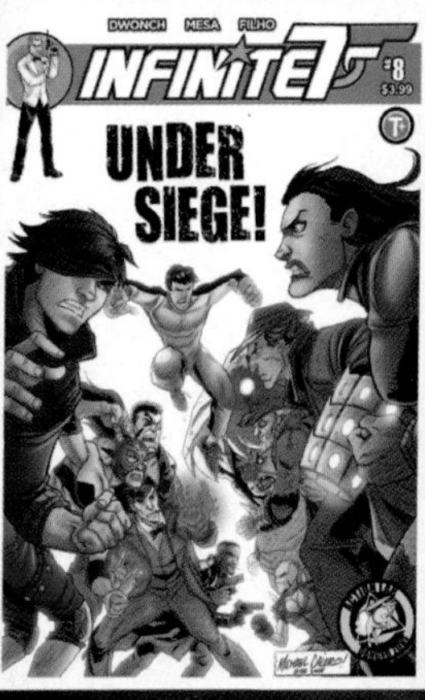

CVR C- ARTIST VARIANT
by Michael Calero
Limited to 1,500 Copies

LETTERED BY DAVE DWONCH

EDITED BY MEGAN DOBRANSKY, SCOTT BRADLEY AND SHAWN GABBORIN

Read Volume One Now!
APR171193

THE STORY SO FAR:

Months have passed since the Laughing Skull was captured by the Infinite Seven. Fearing he might reveal their greatest secrets, the terrorist group Chimera has been left with only one option: a declaration of war.

But will they rescue their agent or simply kill him? And what role will the double agent, Lord Ellington, play?

Read on, true believers...

ACTION LABCOMICS.COM

JASON MARTIN - PUBLISHER
BRYAN SEATON - CEO
SHAWN PRYOR - PRESIDENT
SHAWN GABBORIN - EDITOR IN CHIEF
NICOLE D'ANDRIA - MARKETING MGR.
JIM DIETZ - SOCIAL MEDIA DIRECTOR
CHAD CICCONI - MORE MACHINE THAN MAN

CHAPTER EIGHT

UNDER SIEGE

NEXT ISSUE:

HE WILL BE SET FREE.

COVER GALLERY

COVERS A & B BY ARTURO MESA

COVER C BY ANDREW HERMAN

ONE MONTH LATER.

GOD DAMN IT!

TELL AUTUMN I WANT TO SEE HER. TELL HER I'M READY.
NEXT: UNDER SIEGE

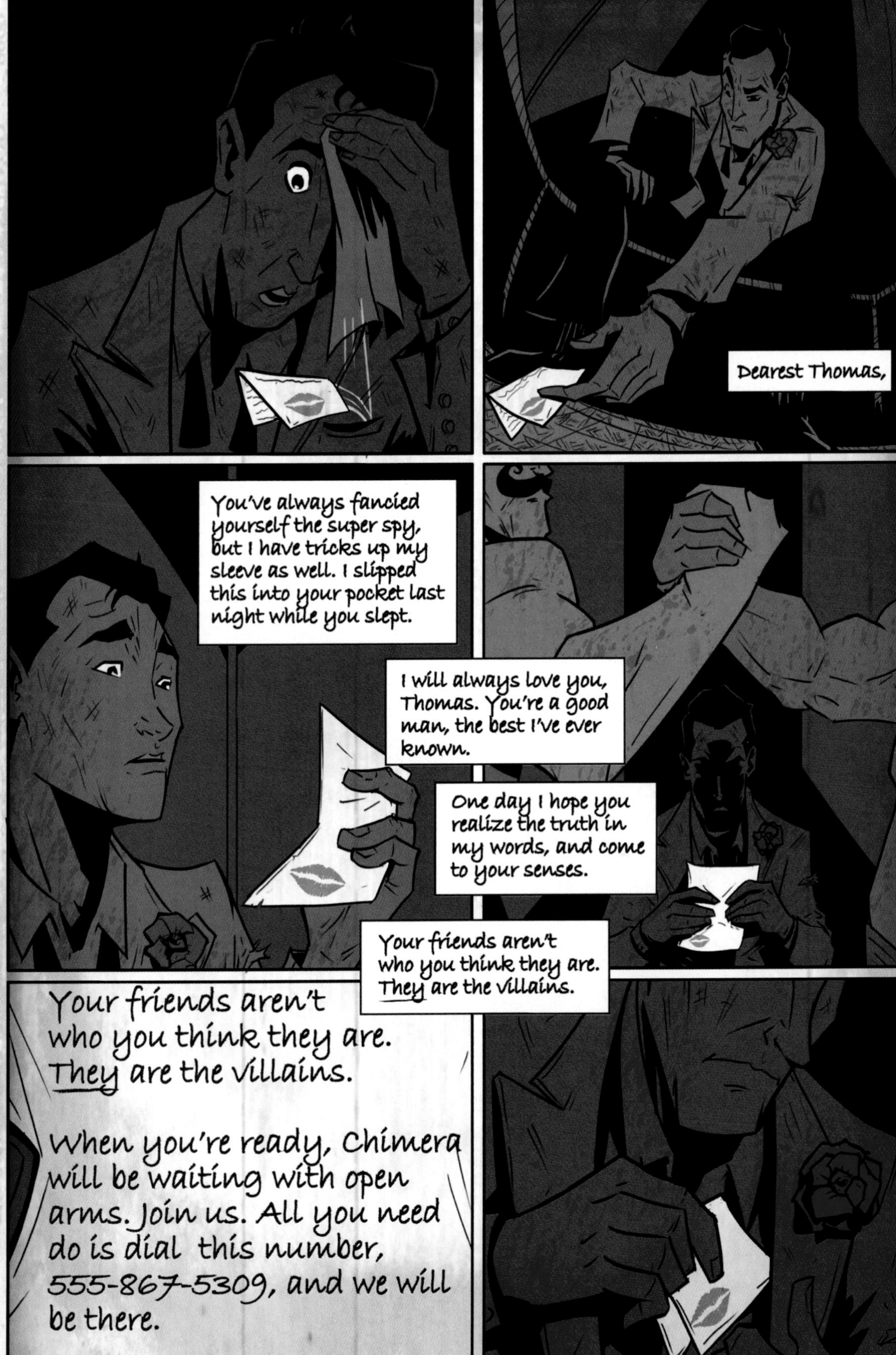

Dearest Thomas,
You've always fancied yourself the super spy, but I have tricks up my sleeve as well. I slipped this into your pocket last night while you slept.
I will always love you, Thomas. You're a good man, the best I've ever known.
One day I hope you realize the truth in my words, and come to your senses.
Your friends aren't who you think they are. They are the villains.
Your friends aren't who you think they are. They are the villains.
When you're ready, Chimera will be waiting with open arms. Join us. All you need do is dial this number, 555-867-5309, and we will be there.
Your Always, Autumn.

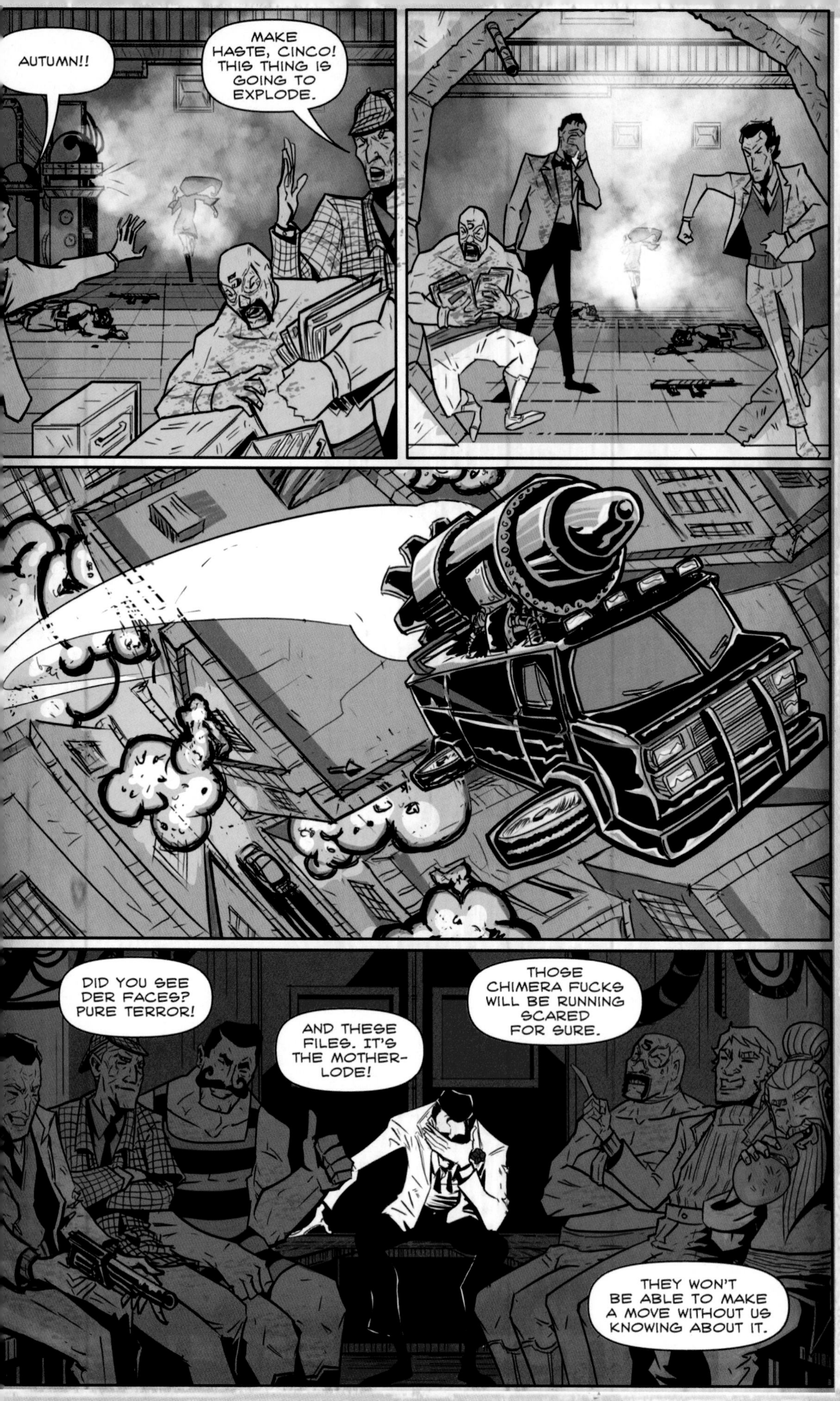
AUTUMN!!
MAKE HASTE, CINCO! THIS THING IS GOING TO EXPLODE.
DID YOU SEE DER FACES? PURE TERROR!
AND THESE FILES. IT'S THE MOTHER-LODE!
THOSE CHIMERA FUCKS WILL BE RUNNING SCARED FOR SURE.
THEY WON'T BE ABLE TO MAKE A MOVE WITHOUT US KNOWING ABOUT IT.

DOESN'T SHE KNOW VEE AREN'T TO HARM HER?

YOU GOT ME, BUT IF SOMEONE IS GOING TO TAKE A SHOT AT ME...

...WELL, I FIGURE I'M GONNA RETURN THE FAVOR.

FSSSSSS

PING

ARGHH!

"--I'LL KILL YOU MYSELF."
REMEMBER WHAT I SAID. THE GIRL STAYS *ALIVE.*

--DON'T BE LATE."
ABOUT TIME, YOU FUCKING TWATS.
ALWAYS SO SENSITIVE. I SWEAR TO GOD, YOU'RE SUCH A PUSSY-
ENOUGH!
THIS WAS GOING TO BE A SIMPLE SMASH UP.
NO WITNESSES, NO CASUALTIES. NOW... NOW WE'RE LOOKING DOWN ON A BLOOD BATH!
YOU'VE NEVER HAD A PROBLEM WITH DEALING DEATH, ELLINGTON.
ARE YOU KEEPING SECRETS FROM US? FEELINGS FOR ANOTHER, PERHAPS?
LISTEN, YOU PERCEPTIVE TOAD, I DON'T NEED TO JUSTIFY MYSELF TO ANY OF YOU. BUT KNOW THIS:
THERE IS A WOMAN DOWN THERE. AND IF ONE HAIR IS HARMED ON HER HEAD--

I KNOW. TOMORROW YOU'LL GO BACK TO YOUR WORLD, AND I BACK TO MINE.

SHIPS IN THE NIGHT.

RIGHT.

MMMM... I HAD HOPED THAT WE MIGHT BE ABLE TO DO THAT AGAIN SOMETIME, BUT ALAS...

THE NIGHT IS STILL YOUNG, DARLING. LET'S NOT RUIN IT WITH TALK.

OH, THOMAS.

HOURS LATER.
TELEPHONE

IT'S ELLINGTON. ASSEMBLE THE TEAM. WE NEED TO TAKE THE BASE TONIGHT.
AFFIRMATIVE. RENDEZVOUS AT TH STRIKE ZONE. AND AGENT SEVEN--

WE'VE BEEN WATCHING YOU. I'VE BEEN WATCHING YOU. YOU'RE A GOOD PERSON, THOMAS.
YOU HAVE DIRECT ACCESS TO THE SHADOW CABINET.
I- WE NEED A MAN LIKE YOU. WE COULD SAVE HUMANITY.
"THIS DOESN'T CHANGE A THING, YOU KNOW."

THIS ISN'T A GAME. PEOPLE HAVE DIED, AUTUMN.
YOU'RE ONE TO TALK, "LORD ELLINGTON." YOUR BAND OF THUGS HAVE BEEN MURDERING INNOCENT PEOPLE FOR YEARS.
TELL ME ABOUT THE WEAPON YOU'RE BUILDING.
W-WEAPON? YOU'VE GOT IT ALL WRONG, WE-
DON'T MAKE ME HURT YOU, GIRL.
AS IF YOU COULD HURT ME ANY MORE THAN YOU ALREADY HAVE.
THE WORLD IS GOING TO HELL, THOMAS. THE EXPLOITATION OF RESOURCES, CLIMATE CHANGE, CIVIL UNREST—THE THREAT IS REAL. WE'RE ON THE BRINK OF SELF-DESTRUCTION
CHIMERA IS A THINK TANK, TASKED WITH SAVING HUMANITY BY ANY MEANS NECESSARY. THIS WORLD IS DOOMED, AND SO WE ARE LOOKING TO THE STARS. WE'RE NOT BUILDING A WEAPON, THOMAS.
WE'RE BUILDING A DEVICE THAT CREATES HABITABLE WORLDS FOR COLONIZATION. WE CALL IT OPERATION: SPACE SEED.
NONSENSE. SCIENCE FICTION AT BEST.
IT'S THE TRUTH. AND YOUR BOSSES, THE SHADOW CABINET, THEY WOULD DO ANYTHING TO STOP US.
THEY NEED HUMANITY TO LIVE IN FEAR. WITHOUT HOPE. IT'S MAKES THEM EASIER TO CONTROL.

"UNDER NO CIRCUMSTANCE ARE YOU TO ENGAGE THE ENEMY."

HELLO, THOMAS.
OR IS IT LORD ELLINGTON THESE DAYS?

WHICHEVER YOU PREFER, AUTUMN. IT SEEMS THAT WE'RE ALL LEADING DOUBLE LIVES THESE DAYS.
HOW LONG?
WHISKEY

COME AGAIN?
HOW LONG HAVE YOU BEEN WORKING FOR THEM. FOR CHIMERA?

OH, THOMAS. DO YOU REALLY WANT TO KNOW THE DETAILS?
I'VE BEEN AN AGENT OF CHIMERA FOR YEARS. THE THINGS WE'VE ACCOMPLISHED...

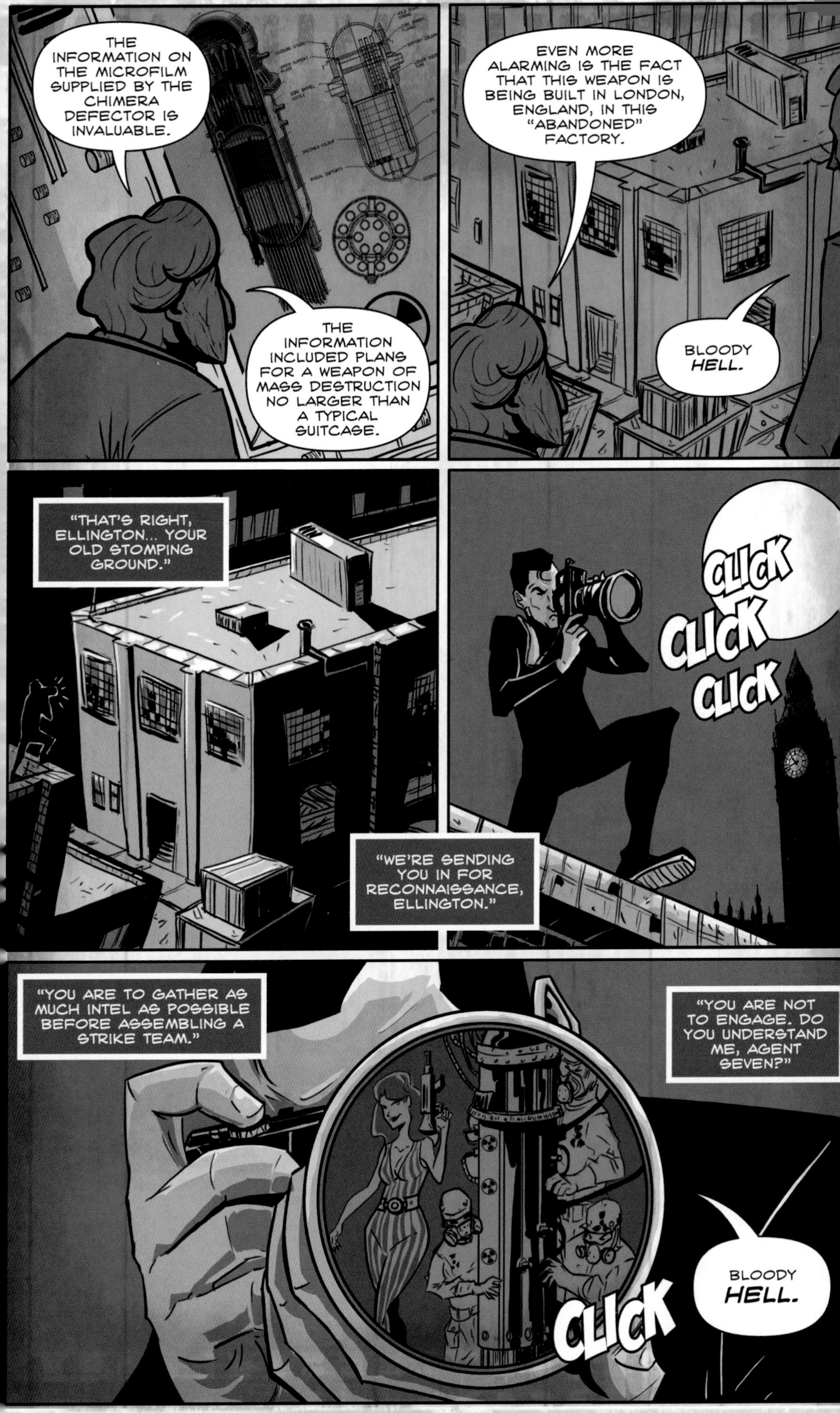
THE INFORMATION ON THE MICROFILM SUPPLIED BY THE CHIMERA DEFECTOR IS INVALUABLE.
THE INFORMATION INCLUDED PLANS FOR A WEAPON OF MASS DESTRUCTION NO LARGER THAN A TYPICAL SUITCASE.
EVEN MORE ALARMING IS THE FACT THAT THIS WEAPON IS BEING BUILT IN LONDON, ENGLAND, IN THIS "ABANDONED" FACTORY.
BLOODY HELL.
"THAT'S RIGHT, ELLINGTON... YOUR OLD STOMPING GROUND."
CLICK
CLICK
CLICK
"WE'RE SENDING YOU IN FOR RECONNAISSANCE, ELLINGTON."
"YOU ARE TO GATHER AS MUCH INTEL AS POSSIBLE BEFORE ASSEMBLING A STRIKE TEAM."
"YOU ARE NOT TO ENGAGE. DO YOU UNDERSTAND ME, AGENT SEVEN?"
CLICK
BLOODY HELL.

AND SOON.

BRILLIANT JOB OUT THERE, TEAM. BOTH ALPHA AND I-

STOW IT, OMEGA. TACTICAL WAS FUCKED FROM THE GET GO.

YOU DROPPED US INTO A MEAT GRINDER. WE NEARLY DIED OUT THERE!

YES, WELL, IT WAS IMPERATIVE THAT WE MOVED WHEN WE DID. THE WINDOW OF EXTRACTION WAS-
WHATEVER.
IT'S NOT YOUR ASS ON THE LINE.
FROM NOW ON, WE PLAN OUR OWN MISSIONS.

WE WILL TAKE THAT UNDER CONSIDERATION, AGENT SIX, NOW PLEASE LEAVE OMEGA BE.
WE HAVE MUCH TO DISCUSS.

I MEANT NO DISRESPECT, ALPHA.
NONE TAKEN. LET'S GET TO BUSINESS, SHALL WE?

OMEGA, IF YOU WOULD?
YES, SIR.

THANK GOD. YOU GOT MY MESSAGE.

YES, YES. VERY CLEVER, I KNOW.
DO YOU HAVE IT?

Y-YES. THEY- CHIMERA PLAN TO DEVASTATE THE WORLD ECONOMY. IT- IT'S-

I'M SURE IT'S ALL VERY TERRIBLE, WHATEVER THEY HAVE PLANNED.
BUT LET'S FOCUS ON THE HERE AND NOW, AND GET OUR ASSES THE HELL OUT OF RUSSIA, EH?

THIS MISSION HAS GONE TO SHIT. CHIMERA DEFECTOR MY ASS. WE'VE BEEN SET UP.
I'D AGREE WITH BRANNAGAN, SAVE ONE DETAIL.
WHAT'S THAT, SHERLOCK?
THE LIGHT FROM THAT WINDOW HAS BEEN FLICKERING THE MESSAGE "SAVE ME" IN MORSE CODE SINCE THE FIGHTING BEGAN.
WE'LL COVER YOU. JUST MAKE SURE YOU GET THE PACKAGE TO THE EXTRACTION POINT.
GOOD CATCH, MAN. HOW DID YOU-?
I HAVE AN ATTENTION TO DETAIL. *EVERY DETAIL.*

THIS COULD HAVE GONE MUCH SMOOTHER. YOU GWEILO AND YOUR GUNS.
1974
VAT VAS DAT, ZHEN? I CAN'T HEAR YOU OVER DE GUN FIRE.
EXACTLY. IDIOTS.

WE'VE HAD OUR EYE ON YOU FOR A LONG WHILE. YOU WERE TOP OF YOUR CLASS AT THE ACADEMY...THE ROYAL NAVY... MI-5, BUT YOU'VE ALWAYS HAD A PROBLEM WITH AUTHORITY. YES?
YOU'RE NOT ANSWERING MY QUESTION, FRIEND.
WHAT IF YOU BECAME THE AUTHORITY? *THAT* IS WHY I AM HERE.
I AM CINCO, MEMBER OF THE ***INFINITE SIX.***
AND I AM HERE TO RECRUIT YOU AS OUR SEVENTH AGENT.
THAT... THAT IS A ***FANTASTIC STORY***, REALLY, BUT EVEN IF IT WERE TRUE, WELL, I HAVE A LIFE HERE IN LONDON.
YOU'VE SAID IT YOURSELF: NOTHING IS PERMANENT.
MY, YOU REALLY ***HAVE*** BEEN WATCHING ME.
THIS IS BIGGER THAN ENGLAND, BIGGER THAN ***ANY*** COUNTRY.
IT'S TIME TO FILL THAT VOID IN YOUR LIFE. YOU KNOW YOU'VE FELT IT.
IT'S TIME TO STOP HIDING BEHIND THAT FACADE OF YOURS AND BECOME THE MAN YOU'RE DESTINED TO BE.
WE EVEN HAVE A NEW IDENTITY FOR YOU...

ONE WEEK LATER.

COME IN, CHICO. AND PUT THE PEA SHOOTER AWAY. YOU WON'T NEED IT. WE HAVE A SAYING IN OUR ORGANIZATION--

--IF I WANTED YOU DEAD... *DEAD YOU WOULD BE.*

CUTE. THEN LET ME ASK... WHO THE BLOODY HELL ARE YOU...
...AND WHAT THE FUCK ARE YOU DOING IN APARTMENT?

WELL, THAT DOESN'T SOUND PLEASANT.
THOMAS, I'M WORRIED FOR YOU.
I'LL BE FINE, AUTUMN.
I'M BEING SERIOUS.
YOU NEED TO WATCH YOUR BACK, THOMAS. WE ARE LIVING IN DANGEROUS TIMES. THERE ARE RUMORS THAT CHIMERA HAS SLEEPER AGENTS EVERYWHERE. NO ONE CAN BE TRUSTED.
YOU ASSUME THAT I TRUST *ANYONE*, DEAR. I'M A SURVIVOR, PLAIN AND SIMPLE.
I DON'T WANT TO LOSE YOU.
OH, DEAR GIRL. NOTHING IS PERMANENT, ESPECIALLY IN OUR LINE OF WORK.
DON'T LET YOUR WOMANLY EMOTIONS CLOUD *THAT* FACT.
PIG!

OF COURSE. I DISPENSE ALL NARRATIVES WHILE YOU'RE COMATOSE, MCBAIN. IT'S NOT AS IF THE INFORMATION WILL STICK.
VERY EFFICIENT, SIGMA.
THOMAS! YOU'RE AWAKE!
ERK. YES. YES, I AM... AND NOT... NOT QUITE READY FOR AFFECTION, DEAR.
OH! SORRY!
YES, WELL, I'LL LEAVE YOU TWO ALONE. BUT ONE THING, THOMAS...
THE HIGHER UPS ARE VERY DISPLEASED WITH YOUR INSUBORDINATION.
YOU'RE GETTING REASSIGNED.
YOU'LL BE LUCKY IF YOU'RE NOT SENT TO SIBERIA.

CHEEKY BASTARD. DID YOU GET ANY INTEL AT ALL?
NOT MUCH. ***A NAME.*** THE... DOCTOR... GAVE ME... ONLY THAT.

WILL HE BE ALL RIGHT?

WE... WE JUST ***DON'T KNOW.***

HOW HE ESCAPED THAT EXPLOSION IS BEYOND US, AND THE INJURIES SUSTAINED, WELL, HE SHOULDN'T HAVE EVEN BEEN ABLE TO WALK TO THE BEACH.

INCREDIBLE.

INCREDIBLY FOOLISH. THOMAS MCBAIN HAS NEVER BEEN ONE TO FOLLOW ORDERS, BUT TO ENTER THAT SNAKE PIT WITHOUT BACKUP...

BUT NOW WE KNOW WHO WE'RE DEALING WITH. ***CHIMERA.*** IT WON'T BE LONG 'TIL WE'RE KNOCKING ON ***THEIR*** DOORS.

FOR THAT, WE CAN THANK AGENT MCBAIN. STILL, IF HE DOES WAKE, THERE WILL BE HELL TO PAY.

YOU... YOU KNOW I CAN... HEAR YOU, RIGHT SIGMA?

BOOM!
BOOM!
BOOM
NO...
...THOMAS...
YOU KNOW... I WON'T... BE OFFENDED...
...IF YOU BLAMED THOSE TEARS... ON THE SUNLIGHT.
THOMAS! I THOUGHT THAT I...THAT WE'D LOST YOU, I-
I THOUGHT YOU SAID YOU'D PREFER TO KEEP OUR RELATIONSHIP PROFESSIONAL, AUTUMN.
OH, TO HELL WITH IT.
IT LOOKS LIKE AUTUMN IS GOING TO COM EARLY THIS YEAR.

HA HA
COFF COFF
OH, THAT'S RICH
COFF
FORGIVE ME, BUT YOU ARE HILARIOUS, MR. MCBAIN. NO, NO...
...I'M AFRAID I WON'T BE DIVULGING ANYTHING OF OUR CONSORTIUM.
BUT I WILL TELL YOU THIS: WE ARE GOING TO CHANGE THE WORLD.
THUGS, MERCENARIES, TERRORISTS.
YOU FORGET THAT TERRORISTS ARE FREEDOM FIGHTERS, FROM A CERTAIN PERSPECTIVE.
AND THAT IS WHAT WE ARE. WE ARE THE PROTECTORS AT THE GATE. PROTECTORS OF THE FUTURE.
A THREE-HEADED GUARDIAN.
TELL ME. WHO. YOU. WORK. FOR.
AH, WHAT THE HELL, IT DOESN'T MATTER.
WE ARE-

I'M NOT COUNTING...
...BUT YOUR DAYS ARE NUMBERED, DOCTOR ABACUS.
ALWAYS SO SMUG, MCBAIN. THE PISTOL... YOU... WON'T NEED IT.
YOUR C4 HAS MADE SURE I WON'T BE WALKING AWAY FROM HERE ALIVE.
NOW COME, SIT WITH ME.
WE ARE NOT SAVAGES, MCBAIN. SIT. THESE CIGARETTES AREN'T GOING TO SMOKE THEMSELVES.
DON'T MIND IF I DO.
NOW, BEFORE YOU SHUFFLE OFF THIS MORTAL COIL, DOCTOR...
TELL ME WHO YOU WORK FOR.

1972
STEADY, OLD BOY. STEADY.

ACTION LAB DANGER ZONE PRESENTS

INFINITE 7

WRITTEN BY
DAVE DWONCH

DRAWN AND COLORED BY BY
ARTURO MESA

CVR A- MOVIE POSTER
by Arturo Mesa

CVR B-
GOD SAVE THE KING
by Arturo Mesa
Limited to 1,500 Copies

CVR C- ARTIST VARIANT
by Andrew Herman
Limited to 1,500 Copies

LETTERED BY DAVE DWONCH

EDITED BY MEGAN DOBRANSKY AND SHAWN GABBORIN

THE STORY SO FAR:

For years, the terrorist organization Chimera has plagued the world. Hell bent on world domination, the only thing standing in their way is the Shadow Cabinet, and their team of assassins, the Infinite Seven.

Little do the Infinite Seven know that there is a double agent amongst them, a lion among the sheep. One of Chimera's leaders has been a member of their group for more than 30 years. This is his story...

Read Volume One Now!
APR171193

Printed in Canada. First printing.

ACTION LABCOMICS.COM

JASON MARTIN - PUBLISHER
BRYAN SEATON - CEO
SHAWN PRYOR - PRESIDENT
SHAWN GABBORIN - EDITOR IN CHIEF
NICOLE D'ANDRIA - MARKETING MGR.
JIM DIETZ - SOCIAL MEDIA DIRECTOR
CHAD CICCONI - MORE MACHINE THAN MAN

CHAPTER 007

THE MAGNIFICENT SEVEN

NEXT ISSUE
THE HIDDEN TRUTH REVEALED
VILLAIN

PROPERTY OF THE S

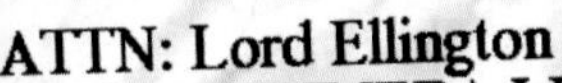

ATTN: Lord Ellington
Subject: CHIMERA LEADER
Date: 03/21/89

FILE 748: THE LION

We have our suspicions that Madame Mavara and The Laughing Skull have not been working alone. If the terrorist organization Chimera is drawing inspiration from the mythical beast, there is a third head.

If Mavara is the serpent, and the Skull the goat, then there MUST be a lion.

We believe the Lion was present at your last mission, and was the person responsible for the death of the Chimera informant as well as the deaths of our extraction team the Hotel Novotel.

Your team must find this monster and elimate them. Failure is unacceptable, Agent Seven. We expect this matter resolved within the week.

OMEGA

PROPERTY OF THE SHADOW CABINET

Subject: Rutherford Zane, The Laughing Skull (ALIAS)
Date: 05/28/17

Details: The man known as The Laughing Skull has been a thorn in our sides for years. Until recently, his identity was a mystery, but in the battle of Chimera Island, he was revealed to be Rutherford Zane, the father of the newest Smash Brannagan. More incredibly still, when unmasked Rutherford had no recollection of the evil acts he's committed as the Skull.

We now have him under observation at HQ and will extract as much intel as possible. It's only a matter of time before he breaks. Who knows what secrets will be revealed when he does?

I am concerned for Smash Brannagan, however. Knowing that his father is a madman, and his mother is the head of Chimera (SEE: Madame Mavara file) has driven him to revenge. While he has become quite formidable, I fear his judgement could become clouded.

Lord Ellington
I7 Field Leader

FILE 001: AGENT SHERLOCK

PROPERTY OF THE SHA

Subject: Mycroft Holmes, Sherlock (ALIAS)
Date: 07/22/17

Details: Mycroft Holmes was the last son born into the famed Holmes family. He was just as brilliant as the name would imply, his skills as a detective unrivaled. But as with all the Holmes boys, he fell prey to the one thing he could not comprhend: Magic.

The Moriarty Clan had been practicing the dark arts for centuries before James Moriarty revealed their secret to Mycroft Holmes, who seemingly perished in their last battle.

Now our old friend Mycroft has returned, enhanced by those Chimera bastards. He clearly has an agenda all his own, but the technology that saved him has also made him a slave to the terrorist group that he once fought. We will do our best to save him, but I fear what path he will choose once his shackles are broken. Will he be friend or foe? And what does this mean for James Moriarty, the current Sherlock? Only time will tell.

Lord Ellington
I7 Field Leader

Viaduktstrasse
Letten-Viadukt
Kindertreffpunkt im
Viadukt Bogen 16
Josefstrasse
Kuoni Cruises
Josefwiese
Supermarket
Hive

COVER GALLERY

A: REGULAR COVER BY ARTURO MESA AND GERALDO FILHO

B: MOVIE POSTER VARIANT BY ARTURO MESA AND GERALDO FILHO

C: ARTIST VARIANT BY JOSH GREATHOUSE

--THAT LORD ELLINGTON HAS BEEN PLAYING THEM FOR FOOLS FROM THE START!
ASSEMBLE YOUR STRIKE TEAM.
WE GO TO WAR IN THE MORNING!
NEXT: THE MAGNIFICENT SEVEN

YOUR CYBORG IS IN NO CONDITION TO MOUNT AN ASSAULT ON THE INFINITE SEVEN'S HIDDEN BASE. WE ARE ON A SCHEDULE, AND TIME IS RUNNING OUT!
HE'LL BE READY.
WE ARE WIPING HIS MEMORY BANKS NOW.
HE *WILL* BE READY.
HE BLOODY WELL BETTER BE.
THE MORE TIME THE LAUGHING SKULL IS A PRISONER, THE GREATER CHANCE HIS MEMORIES WILL EMERGE.
ALL OF OUR DIRTY SECRETS WILL BE BROUGHT INTO THE LIGHT.
TSSK. I'D HATE TO LOSE MY FAVORITE PLAYTHING.
HE' A LIABILITY THAT MUST BE *ELIMINATED.*
IF HE'S SUCH A PROBLEM, WHY NOT DO IT YOURSELF?
YOU KNOW DAMN WELL WHY *NOT,* WOMAN.
MY IDENTITY MUST REMAIN A SECRET.
THE INFINITE SEVEN CANNOT EVER DISCOVER THAT THE LEADER OF CHIMERA HAS BEEN MANIPULATING THEM FROM THE SHADOWS FOR *YEARS--*

NOW I HAVE A BIT OF PAYBACK TO DELIVER.
I'M GOING TO FIND THE PEOPLE THAT DID THIS TO ME, AND THEN-
CLICK

THAT IS ENOUGH, CYBORG.
YOU MAY THINK YOU HAVE REGAINED YOUR FREE WILL, BUT CHIMERA IS NOT DONE WITH YOU
YOU ARE OUR SLAVE, BODY AND SOUL.

CHIMERA...

THAT'S RIGHT, BOY. THIS WAS MERELY A TEST.
YOUR MOTHER HAS GREAT THINGS PLANNED FOR YOU... AND YOUR FATHER.
"IF THIS WAS A TEST, IT WAS A BLOODY FAILURE!"

PROGRAM OVERRIDE. CANCELLING PRIMARY DIRECTIVE.
TERMINATION CANCELLED.
I REALLY SHOULD THANK YOU, BOYS.
WITHOUT YOU I WOULDN'T HAVE BEEN ABLE TO REGAIN THESE MEMORIES. BUT TO BE HONEST...
B-BUNNY...
KRAK
I DON'T TRUST *ANY* OF YOU.

CAUSE OF DEATH UNCLEAR. IMPACT OR DROWNING. HE-
NO, MYCROFT... YOU'RE ALIVE...
...AND WE'VE MISSED YOU TERRIBLY.
I... I
I- I- I... REMEMBER.
BZZZZZZZz

DESIGNATE:
MASTER ZHEN.
THREAT LEVEL: 78%.
ELIMINATE.
COME ON, WE HAVE TO SAVE-
NO. LET ME TALK TO HIM.
DO YOU REMEMBER WHO YOU WERE? DO YOU REMEMBER, MYCROFT?
MY...
MYCROFT HOLMES.
SEARCHING. SEARCHING.
LAST IN THE HOLMES LINEAGE PLUMMETED TO HIS DEATH ON OCTOBER 27TH, 2015.

KRA-KOOM!
TARGETS ASSESSED.
OH, SHIT.
DESIGNATE: SHERLOCK. THREAT LEVEL 98%.
TARGET FOR ELIMINATION.
NO.
NOW WE FINISH THIS.

BLAM
BLAM
BLAM
BLAM

SPLACK!!!

THOK!

WHAT? IT WAS ALL I COULD FIND!

KRAK
"ZHEN IS THE ONE OPENING THE WINDOW."
HAI!!!
PUNCH
PUNCH
PUNCH
PUNCH
PUNCH
NOW!
BOOM

SPEAK FOR YOURSELF. I AM ALWAYS READY TO DELIVER PAIN.
WHERE THE HELL DID YOU HIDE THOSE???
YOU DON'T WANT TO KNOW.
FOOM!
AND WHAT THE HELL ARE YOU DOING? NOW'S NOT THE TIME TO DRINK, WASHINGTON!
OH, GROW UP. THIS AIN'T FOR ME. IT'S FOR HIM.
WE'RE GONNA HAVE A SMALL WINDOW TO TAKE THIS SUCKA DOWN. ONE CHANCE, YOU FEEL ME?
FINE. SURE. BUT WHERE IS ZHEN? SHOULD WE FIND HIM FIRST?
C'MON, KID...

BUNNY? WHAT HAVE THEY DONE TO YOU?

FOOM!
MY, YOU HAVE ***CHANGED***. CAN'T SAY I'M NOT AROUSED.

WHAT THE HELL IS GOING ON? WHO IS ***THAT?***
JUDGING BY THE PILLOW TALK, IT MUST BE THE ***OTHER*** SHERLOCK.
THE LAST GUY?! I THOUGHT HE DIED?
SHIT LIKE THIS HAPPENS ALL THE TIME.
PEOPLE COME BACK FROM THE DEAD, FRIENDS BECOME ENEMIES, BLAH, BLAH, AND THE WHEEL GOES 'ROUND.
BUT WHAT DO WE DO? WE DON'T HAVE ANY WEAPONS!

CLANK!
FOOM!
GUN-URK!
TARGETS CONFIRMED.
EXTERMINATE WITH EXTREME PREJUDICE.
FOOM!
FOOM!
FOOM!

YES. THE LAST WARLORD TO HOST THE TOURNAMENT... **BUBALUS**... WAS AN EVIL MAN.
HE USED THE TOURNAMENT AS A FRONT FOR DRUGS, PROSTITUTION.
I... STOPPED HIM.
EVERYONE'S GOT SOB STORIES. MINE IS COVERED IN BLOOD AND BETRAYAL, BUT FUCK IT. LIFE IS FOR THE *LIVING*.
I SUGGEST WE START LIVIN' IT. LET'S GET TO THE *GOOD STUFF*.
YO, WHAT'S IT TAKE TO GET SOME HENNESSY IN THIS BITCH? **WAITRESS!**
ALL THESE CLUBS ARE THE SAME. SHIT SERVICE, AM I RIGHT?
VAT IS-

IT'S NOT ALWAYS DOOM AND GLOOM, ANTH... SMASH. THE GENERAL RULE IS TO KILL A MEMBER TO BECOME ONE, BUT THE TITLE WOLFSBERG HAS BEEN IN MY FAMILY FOR YEARS..

YOU SEE, WHEN ONE BECOMES... *AGED*... THE TITLE IS HANDED DOWN TO THE NEXT MOST CAPABLE.

IT'S A LOOPHOLE IN THE SYSTEM, AND VERY EFFECTIVE. MY FAMILY TRAINS FROM BIRTH.

I THOUGHT IT WAS KILL, REPLACE, KILL?
MOSTLY, YES, BUT THERE ARE OTHER WAYS TO BECOME BEST OF THE BEST.

NONE FOR ME.
FOR A TIME, ONCE EVERY TEN YEARS, ON A PRIVATE ISLAND IN THE PACIFIC, THERE WAS A TOURNAMENT TO DETERMINE THE NEXT MASTER ZHEN.

FOR A TIME?

"...WHERE WE'RE GOING THEY ARE GOING TO *LOVE* YOU."
ZURICH, SWITZERLAND. THE HIVE.
LET'S GET YOU A DRINK, EH, BRANNAGAN!
SURE, WHATEVER.
ALWAYS SO **EMO**. PLENTY IN HERE WILL GO FOR ***THAT***.

YOU REALLY NEED TO STOP WITH THAT SHIT. I'M NOT A WALKING BONER.
SURE, I HAVE NEEDS, BUT I...MY HEART IS SET ON SOMEONE.
KISS
AND I HAVE A ***LOT*** TO ***WORK THROUGH***.

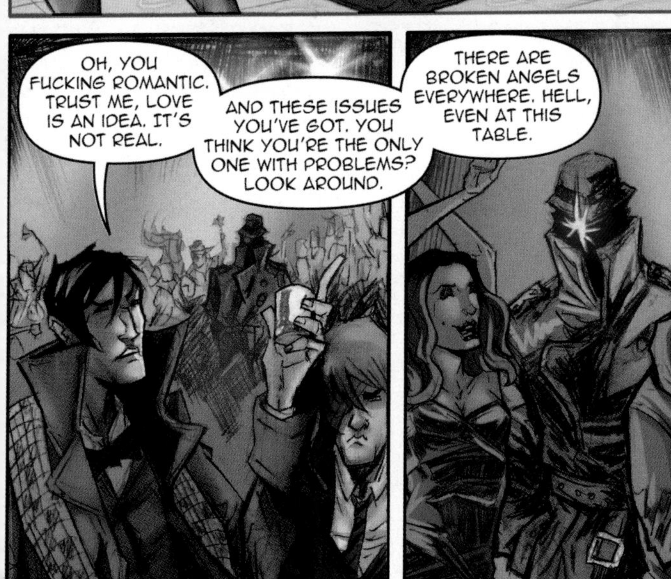

OH, YOU FUCKING ROMANTIC. TRUST ME, LOVE IS AN IDEA. IT'S NOT REAL.
AND THESE ISSUES YOU'VE GOT. YOU THINK YOU'RE THE ONLY ONE WITH PROBLEMS? LOOK AROUND.
THERE ARE BROKEN ANGELS EVERYWHERE. HELL, EVEN AT THIS TABLE.

YOU KNOW WHAT? YOU'RE RIGHT. IN ALL THE INSANITY THIS PAST YEAR...
...I'VE NEVER ONCE GOTTEN TO KNOW YOU GUYS. I HAVE NO IDEA HOW YOU ALL ENDED UP IN THE INFINITE SEVEN.

"--WE HAVE PEOPLE WAITING ON US!"
ABOUT TIME, BIRTHDAY BOY. LET'S GET OUR BOOGIE ON!
JESUS CHRIST.
WHY NOT INVITE ELLINGTON AND CINCO WHILE YOU'RE AT IT???
ELLINGTON ISN'T MUCH OF A CLUB GOER, AND CINCO, WELL, SHE'S STILL RECOVERING FROM, YOU KNOW...
BUT TONIGHT'S NOT ABOUT THAT. TONIGHT'S ABOUT YOU! IS THE JUMP-SHIP PREPPED, WASH?
YOU KNOW IT.
SLAP!
TOPS!
UH, WHERE ARE WE GOING? AM I UNDER-DRESSED?
NOT AT ALL...

DON'T BEAT HIM UP, SMASH.
HE JUST ASKED WHAT I WAS DOING TONIGHT. I'M HITTING THE CLUB.
A LITTLE R&R, AND YOU'RE COMING *WITH*. WE'VE GOT A LOT TO CELEBRATE.
CELEBRATE?
OH. YOU DON'T-? *YOU DON'T REMEMBER?*
TODAY IS YOUR *EIGHTEENTH BIRTHDAY*, SMASH.
I-- I... IT DOESN'T MATTER.
OH, BUT IT DOES! TODAY YOU'RE A *MAN!*
LET'S GET YOU *LAID!*
THAT'S NOT-- THAT'S NOT WHAT I WANT.
BUT IT'S WHAT YOU NEED. WE ALL NEED A RELEASE, BRANNAGAN. UNCLE SHERLOCK KNOWS BEST IN ALL AFFAIRS OF THE FLESH AND SPIRIT, TRUST ME.
WHAT YOU NEED IS A LITTLE PLEASURE TO GET YOUR MIND OFF ALL THIS... *PAIN.**
*LITERALLY! READ ISSUE #5 --DAVE
FINE. FINE.
BRILLIANT! NOW LET'S GET YOU INTO SOMETHING PRESENTABLE. BUT MAKE IT QUICK--

NOW.
YOU HAVE BEEN IN THIS STATE FOR SEVERAL HOURS, SIR.
MIND YOUR BUSINESS, PARROT.
YOU ARE MY BUSINESS, SMASH BRANNAGAN. IF YOU NEED AN EAR, MY RECEPTORS ARE HERE FOR Y-
JESUS, MAN. WHO DESIGNED YOU, DR. PHIL?
SADLY, NO, THOUGH I HAVE BEEN UPGRADED TO SEEM MORE HUMAN.
SEVERAL PROGRAMMERS ARE RESPONSIBLE FOR MY SOURCE CODE. IN 1983, BETA PARROT NEARLY STARTED WORLD WAR 3, AND-
I DON'T CARE, PARROT. JUST LEAVE ME ALONE. I'M FINE.
I'M SORRY, SIR, BUT THAT CONFLICTS WITH MY PRIMARY FUNCTION. TO THAT END, I'VE ORGANIZED-
HELLLLLO?
IS HE READY THEN, PARROT? THE NIGHT IS YOUNG.
OH, GOD. WHAT DID YOU DO, PARROT?

ONE MONTH AGO.

YOU'RE SURE HE IS ONLINE? THAT HE CAN HEAR ME?

YES, MADAME MAVARA.

AND VIDEO? HE CAN SEE ME?

YES, MA'AM.

EXCELLENT. YOU'RE IN THERE, AREN'T YOU, ARCHIE?
GOOD, *GOOD*.
SCANNING...

YOUR FRIENDS... THEY NEVER WERE. WE RESCUED YOU. REBUILT YOU.

AND WE WILL GIVE YOU PURPOSE. NOT THE CAT AND MOUSE GAME YOU'VE PLAYED IN THE PAST.

IDENTIFIED: MADAME MAVARA

YOU WILL BE MY ANGEL OF DEATH, AND THEY WILL FEAR YOUR NAME.

CYBORG

STORY: DAVE DWONCH ART: ARTURO MESA
COLORS: GERALDO FILHO LETTERS: DAVE DWONCH

TWO MONTHS AGO.
RESPECT. HONOR. TRADITION.
HE THREATENED ALL OF THAT. ALL OF THIS.
But he did not... take it.
NO, HE TOOK MUCH MORE THAN THAT, BUBALUS, DIDN'T HE?
Hmnn.
YOU WERE ONCE THE GREATEST WARRIOR IN THE EAST. A CELEBRATED GENERAL. NOW JUST A BROKEN MAN. HE DID THIS TO YOU.
WOULD YOU NOT HAVE YOUR REVENGE?
I- I cannot.
IT BURNS IN YOUR HEART. LET ME GIVE YOU RELEASE.
GIVE ME YOUR TEN BEST. WE WILL AVENGE YOU.
yes.

THREE MONTHS AGO.
YOU USED TO NOT NEED THE SCOPE, OLD MAN.
WE ALL GET OLD. THE SIGHT GOES FIRST.
YOU'RE NOT LOOKING ANY YOUNGER TO ME, BITCH.
ALWAYS THE CHARMER, HANS. IT MUST BE HARD, BEING PUT OUT TO PASTURE. TO BE REPLACED BY THE YOUNGER MODEL.
I'VE MADE MY PEACE. WHAT DO YOU WANT?
TO GIVE YOU THE RESPECT YOU DESERVE. REVENGE. POWER. YOUR NAME.
WHAT DO YOU SAY, WOLFSBERG?
TELL ME MORE.

FOUR MONTHS AGO.
HELLO, SKULL.
Who-who are you?
YOU KNOW DAMN WELL WHO I AM, BASTARD.
I... I'm sorry, but I really don't know you. Is... is my son alright?
HE SURVIVED, NO THANKS TO YOUR BITCH WIFE.
BUT THAT'S NOT WHAT I CAME HERE FOR. I WANT TO TALK TO YOU ABOUT MY FATHER.
I'm sorry. I don't know him, or you. I-
LIAR! YOU MURDERED MY FATHER. YOU KNOW IN YOUR HEART WHAT YOU DID!
BAM
I didn't, I swear! It-it was the mask that-that-
LISTEN TO ME, OLD MAN.
IT MAY TAKE A WEEK, A MONTH... PERHAPS A YEAR, BUT YOU WILL REMEMBER.
AND WHEN YOU DO, I WILL MAKE SURE YOU LIVE LONG ENOUGH TO REGRET WHAT YOU'VE DONE TO MY FAMILY.

ACTION LAB DANGER ZONE PRESENTS

INFINITE 7

WRITTEN BY
DAVE DWONCH

DRAWN BY
ARTURO MESA

COLORED BY
GERALDO FILHO

CVR A- REGULAR COVER
by Arturo Mesa

CVR B- MOVIE POSTER
by Arturo Mesa
Limited to 1,500 Copies

CVR C- ARTIST VARIANT
by Josh Greathouse
Limited to 1,500 Copies

LETTERED BY **DAVE DWONCH**

EDITED BY **MEGAN DOBRANSKY** AND **SHAWN GABBORIN**

THE STORY SO FAR:

Anthony Zane emerged from a three month coma a changed man. Dedicating his life to bringing his mothe, the evil Madame Mavara to justice, Smash dedicated his life to filling the shoes of the previous Smash Brannagan.

His training was put to the test when he faced off ainst fellow I7 member, Cinco, who was sent to eliminate a loose end from Anthony's past, Melanie Dupree.

While he was able to save Melanie, both Anthony and Cinco were left with battle scars...

Read Volume One Now!
APR171193

ACTION LABCOMICS.COM

JASON MARTIN - PUBLISHER
BRYAN SEATON - CEO
SHAWN PRYOR - PRESIDENT
SHAWN GABBORIN - EDITOR IN CHIEF
NICOLE D'ANDRIA - MARKETING MGR.
JIM DIETZ - SOCIAL MEDIA DIRECTOR
CHAD CICCONI - MORE MACHINE THAN MAN

CHAPTER SIX

CYBORG

NEXT ISSUE:

THE PAST WILL HUNT THEM.

FILE 006: SMASH BRANNAGAN

F THE SHADOW CABINET

Subject: Anthony Zane, Smash Brannagan (ALIAS)
Date: 06/09/17

Details: Much has happened to our newest Smash Brannagan, young Anthony Zane. His parents were revealed to be the international terrorists, Madame Mavara and The Laughing Skull. While we were able to apprehend the second, Mavara has eluded capture. Still, her intentions are clear-- world domination, and woe to anyone who stands in her way. This fact was perfectly illustrated as Mavara attempted to kill her own son, sending Anthony into a coma via a bloody bullet to the head.

Anthony spent three months clinging to life and has emerged a changed man, dedicating himself to his training. He has only one purpose now: revenge. I'm certain this new path is something we will be able to exploit in the future. Very soon Smash Brannagan will be the perfect weapon. We can thank his parents for that.

Speaking of... I'm uncertain of if, and when, we should inform the lad of his true lineage. Perhaps the truth will stoke the fire in his heart or tip his mind into insanity. I leave it to your judgement, Alpha. Clearly, my judgement is clouded on the matter.

Lord Ellington
I7 Field Leader

5

COVER GALLERY

A: REGULAR COVER BY
ARTURO MESA & GERALDO FILHO

B: MOVIE POSTER VARIANT
BY ARTURO MESA & GERALDO FILHO

C: ARTIST VARIANT BY
DAVE DWONCH

A- ANTHONY?

GO BACK INSIDE, MELANIE. GO BACK TO BED, AND FORGET YOU EVER KNEW ANTHONY ZANE.

ANTHONY, WHERE HAVE YOU *BEEN?* THAT NIGHT YOU DISAPPEARED, I-

I SAID FORGET YOU EVER KNEW ANTHONY ZANE.

BUT-

IF I HEAR YOU ARE LOOKING FOR HIM, I'LL BE BACK, AND I'LL KILL YOU *MYSELF*.

ANTHONY ZANE IS *DEAD.*

NEXT: CYBORG

WHY?!
WHY WOULD YOU TAKE HER AWAY FROM ME?!
NOT EVEN HER! THE IDEA OF HER!
A BETTER TOMORROW.
WHAT MIGHT HAVE BEEN. WHAT COULD BE.
HOPE.
WHY WOULD YOU TAKE THAT AWAY FROM ME?
WHY?!
TO SAVE YOU.
I DIDN'T WANT YOU TO... TO LIVE WITH THE GUILT, ANTHONY.
HER MURDER WOULD... KILL YOU INSIDE. YOU NEED TO LIVE...
BUT YOU HAVE TO LET HER GO. FOR HER SAKE... AS WELL AS YOURS...

YOU'LL DISCOVER I'M FULL OF SURPRISES, CABRON. THE GIRL DIES TONIGHT.
OVER MY DEAD BODY.
THAT CAN BE ARRANGED.

"THE RED PILL CLEARS IT RIGHT UP!"
MISSING
I WON'T LET YOU DO IT. I'LL STOP YOU, EVEN IF IT MEANS KILLING YOU.
OH, ANTHONY--
--DO YOU REALLY THINK YOU HAVE A CHANCE OF STOPPING ME? SHE WILL DIE PAINLESSLY, IN HER SLEEP.
IT WILL LOOK LIKE A HEART ATTACK. IMPROBABLE, BUT NOT WHOLLY INCONCEIVABLE.
I FIGURED IT'D BE WASHINGTON, MAYBE MASTER ZHEN. BUT NOT *YOU*.

DON'T TRY PULLING ON MY HEART STRINGS, SMASH. THESE VEINS DRIED UP YEARS AGO.
HOLD THIS, WATSON.
I GOT WHAT Y'NEED, MATE. THE BLUE PILL WILL GET YE WHERE Y'NEED TO GO.
THE RED PILL WILL BRING YOU BACK. ALL YE GOTTA DO IS PICTURE THE PLACE IN YOUR MIND.
SO I JUST SWALLOW THE BLUE PILL, AND-
WHAT ARE YOU, CRACKED?
THAT'D BE THE END OF YE FOR CERTAIN!
YE JUST SMASH THE CAPSULES ON THE GROUND. ANYTHING IN A FIVE-FOOT RADIUS GOES WITH YE. UNDERSTAND?
YEAH! THANKS, SHERLOCK!
SHOULDN'T YE HAVE TOLD 'IM THAT THE BLUE PILL'D GIVE 'IM SYPHILIS?
WHY BOTHER?

FUCK!
FUCK!
FUCK!

FUUUUUUCK!!

SMASH! GOOD T'SEE YOU UP AND ABOUT!
OFF FOR A LITTLE RUMSPRINGA, EH BOYO? GOOD ON YOU!
I NEED A JUMP SHIP, SHERLOCK!

WHAT? NO! I HAVE TO GET TO LEAVENWORTH, KANSAS IN THE NEXT FIVE MINUTES!
NEVER MAKE IT, MATE.
FUCK!!

PLEASE, YOU HAVE TO HELP ME. IF I DON'T GET THERE, SOMEONE... SOMEONE I CARE ABOUT IS GOING TO DIE.
IF YOU COULD GO BACK AND SAVE HIM*, WOULDN'T YOU?!
*SEE ISSUE #3 --DAVE!

I'VE BEEN IN THIS GAME FOR A LONG TIME, SMASH. THEY *NEVER* STOP.
SHE'LL POKE AND PROD, AND BRING DOWN EVERYTHING WE HAVE BUILT.
ARTICLE 45 STATES IT CLEARLY-- ALL TIES MUST BE SEVERED PERSONALLY, PAINLESSLY, AND WITHOUT MERCY.
i don't think i can.
I KNEW YOU'D SAY THAT, WHICH IS WHY I SENT AN AGENT TO DISPOSE OF HER THREE HOURS AGO.
YOUR HANDS WILL BE CLEAN, BOY. BUT YOU'D BETTER LEARN TO *HARDEN UP*.
WE'RE IN THE *BUSINESS OF DEATH*. THERE'S NO ROOM FOR EMOTION.
FUCK.
THERE'S NO ROOM FOR EMOTION, BRANNAGAN!
FUCK!

WE'RE ALL GLAD YOU'RE BACK IN ACTION, SMASH, BUT A LOT HAS HAPPENED IN THE NEARLY EIGHT MONTHS YOU WERE RECUPERATING.
THREATS ABOUND. IN THE SHADOWS AND IN THE LIGHT OF DAY.
IF IT'S CHIMERA, I WANT IN.
EYES TO THE SCREEN, BRANNAGAN. THIS DOESN'T INVOLVE THEM FOR ONCE.
YOU RECOGNIZE THE GIRL?
Melanie.
I FIGURED YOU WOULD. PRETTY THING. SHE'S BECOME A LIABILITY. ONE WE CAN'T AFFORD.
She- SHE'S A GOOD PERSON. HOW-?
BY POKING HER NOSE WHERE IT DOESN'T BELONG.
SHE'S STIRRING THE POT WITH THIS NONSENSE. SHE FANCIES HERSELF A BLOODY DETECTIVE.
MISSING
www.FindAnthonyZane.com
Police Station
HELP
WE ARE A SECRET ORGANIZATION, BRANNAGAN. WE CAN'T HAVE THIS KIND OF ATTENTION.
NANCY FUCKING DREW NEEDS TO GO AWAY, AND YOU'RE GOING TO DO THE DEED.
I- SHE WOULDN'T BE DOING THIS IF IT WEREN'T FOR ME.
I CAN TALK TO HER. MAKE HER STOP.

YOU HEAR ALL THAT?
LOUD AND CLEAR. SEEMS THE HARDER YOU PUSH, THE MORE HE RETREATS.
AND THAT MIND GAME WITH THE MASK... ICE COLD, BRANNAGAN.
CUT THE CRAP, ELLINGTON.
WHAT DO YOU WANT? DO YOU HAVE ANOTHER MISSION FOR ME?
YOU'VE BEEN THROUGH A LOT, SMASH, SO I WILL IGNORE YOUR SHIT ATTITUDE, BUT MY PATIENCE IS WEARING THIN.
DON'T MAKE ME SPANK YOU, LITTLE BOY.
A LITTLE *RESPECT*, AGENT SIX.
FINE, WHATEVER. TELL ME THERE'S A MISSION. WHAT DO YOU HAVE FOR ME?
BE CAREFUL WHAT YOU WISH FOR...

huff... huff...

TELL ME WHERE SHE IS AND I CAN MAKE THIS ALL GO AWAY. TELL ME WHERE *MAVARA* IS.

NO.
I... I don't know.

FINE. PLAY THE FOOL. BUT KNOW THIS:
THE PEOPLE I WORK FOR *WILL* GET WHAT THEY NEED FROM YOU, ONE WAY OR ANOTHER.
SOOON...

AND I'M GOING TO BE THERE WHEN YOU BREAK.

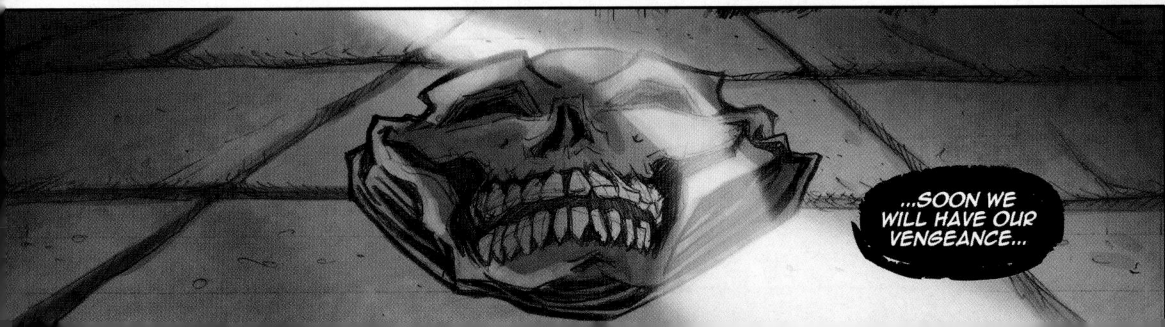

...SOON WE WILL HAVE OUR VENGEANCE...

YOU KNOW WHAT THE SAD THING IS, OLD MAN?
THIS IS ALL BULLSHIT. NONE OF THIS IS REAL.
IT'S A FAKE. *YOU'RE* A FAKE.
Wh... I-
IT'S A FUCKING RUBBER MASK. SOMETHING YOU CAN BUY AT A SHITTY HALLOWEEN STORE.
THE POWERS... THE ELABORATE BACK STORY--
--IT WAS ALL IN YOUR HEAD.
no.
YEAH. YOU'RE JUST A WEAK MAN WHO WOULD DO ANYTHING TO GET IN HER GOOD GRACES.
WELL, SHE DOESN'T GIVE TWO FUCKS ABOUT *YOU*.

Don't let the evil inside of you.

LET'S TEST THAT THEORY, SHALL WE?

No, son! You have no idea what you're doing!

Please! Anthony! It will take hold of you like it did me!!

Puh-please don't do this.

D-don't let it inside you, son.

"...IT'S ONLY A MATTER OF TIME."

HELLO, FATHER.

Anthony! I-

NOT ANYMORE. MY NAME IS SMASH BRANNAGAN.

No, son, they've brain-washed you. You-
YOU'RE ONE TO TALK.
TELL ME ABOUT THE MASK. TELL ME ABOUT THE LAUGHING SKULL.

You... You wouldn't understand.
NO, YOU DON'T UNDERSTAND, DAD.
YOU'RE GOING TO BE LOCKED AWAY IN HERE UNTIL YOU GIVE THEM WHAT THEY NEED. INFORMATION.

NOW TELL ME ABOUT THE GODDAMN MASK.
We found it on a trip through Malaysia. It... It can speak to you... Make you stronger...
If you... If you let it... It can take control of you.

日本
YEAH.
1:15 / 2:23
HAI!!!
THIS GUY COMES OUT OF NOWHERE AND SAVES HIM.
CRUNCH
1:23 / 2:23
IF THAT IS ANTHONY (AND I'M NOT SAYING IT IS)... THEN WHO THE HELL IS THAT GUY?!
TWIST
CRUNCH
TWIST
KRINK
CRUNCH
2:15 / 2:23
I DON'T KNOW. THERE'S NOTHING ONLINE ABOUT HIM. BUT I'M GOING TO MAKE SENSE OF IT...

THERE. SEE? THAT'S *ANTHONY.*

THAT'S A STRETCH, EVEN FOR *YOU,* MELANIE.

IT'S HIM. *I KNOW IT.*

5 Teleportations Caught On Camera & Spotted In Real Life!

Top 5s Finest

4:38

5 Teleportations Caught

Strange Videos

1.740.884 visualizaciones

2:00

I DID SOME RESEARCH.

THE... THING THAT HE WAS FIGHTING... HE WAS SOME SORT OF SUPER-POWERED TERRORIST NAMED THE ***SANDSNAKE***.

GOOGLE HAD WHOLE PAGES ON THE GUY.

THAT GUY IS BAD NEWS.

WAS BAD NEWS. CHECK ***THIS*** OUT.

IS IT TOO MUCH?

IT'S BATSHIT CRAZY, MELANIE. FOR ALL YOU KNOW, HIS PARENTS SURPRISED HIM WITH A TRIP AROUND THE WORLD. THEY ARE INTERNATIONAL BUSINESS TYPES, RIGHT?

I THOUGHT IT WAS CRAZY, TOO. UNTIL I SAW *THIS*.

WHAT?

I'M SHARING THE LINK NOW.

"TO BE HONEST, WE BARELY KNEW EACH OTHER."
"I'D SEEN HIM AROUND, HE WAS SHY... AWKWARD..."
"WE HAD A CONNECTION."
"WE MADE PLANS TO HANG OUT. MOVIE NIGHT AT HIS PLACE, BUT WHEN I GOT THERE HE HAD VANISHED WITHOUT A TRACE."
"ANTHONY AND HIS ENTIRE FAMILY... GONE. AND NO ONE SEEMS TO CARE."
"BUT I DO. I'M GOING TO FIND OUT WHAT HAPPENED TO YOU. I'M GOING TO...

THREE MONTHS LATER.
"WE WEREN'T FRIENDS."
"BUT I KNEW IT INSTANTLY."

ONE MONTH LATER.
huff- huff
sob
COME WITH ME, SMASH BRANNAGAN. NOW IS NOT A TIME FOR TEARS.
YOU MUST FOCUS, OR YOU WILL MISS ALL THE HEAVENLY GLORY.

Hurk!
SLAM

IT'S BEEN THREE MONTHS. HE MUST WAKE UP. WHY HASN'T HE WOKEN UP???
WHAT DO YOU MEAN, CINCO?
HE MAY NEVER, WOLFSBERG. BUT I FEAR FOR THE WORLD IF HE DOES.
YOU HAVE NO IDEA WHAT HAS BEEN GOING THROUGH HIS MIND. THE HATRED HE MUST BE FEELING.
THAT BITCH MAVARA BETTER WATCH HER BACK.
AND WOE TO ANYONE WHO GETS IN HIS WAY. HE MAY NOT HAVE BEEN A KILLER BORN, BUT TAKE IT FROM ME, AFTER ALL HE'S ENDURED--
--HE WILL BE.
Gasp-!